a gift for

_____

from

_____

FATHERS

with love

HODDER

MOMENTS INTIMACY LAUGHTER KINSHIP

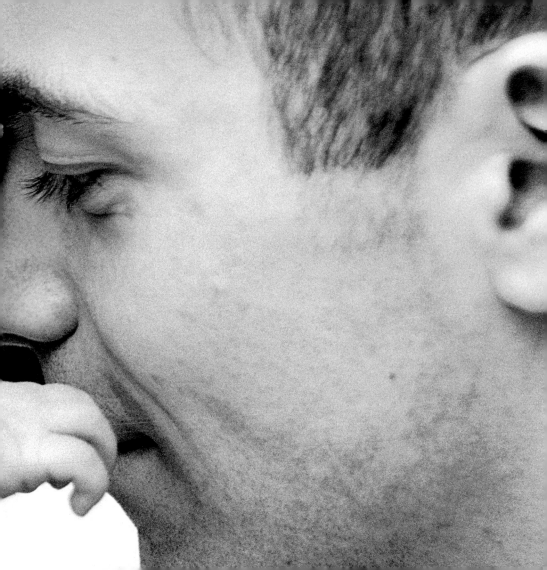

When a child is born, a father is born.

[FREDERICK BUECHNER]

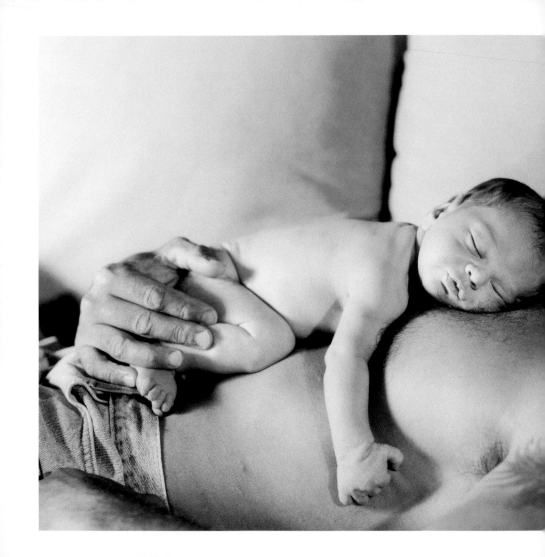

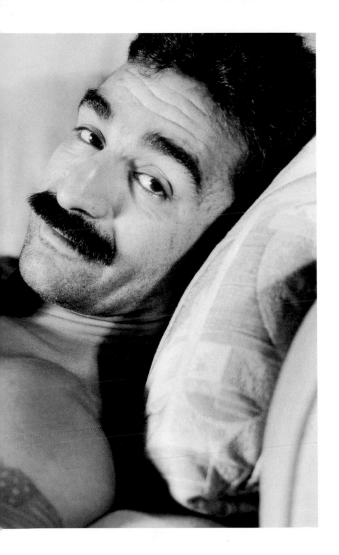

It is not flesh and blood,
but the heart which makes us fathers and sons.

[FRIEDRICH VON SCHILLER]

I do not love him because he is good,
but because he is my little child.

[RABINDRANATH TAGORE]

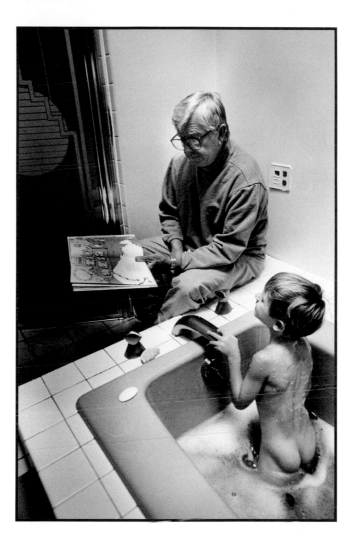

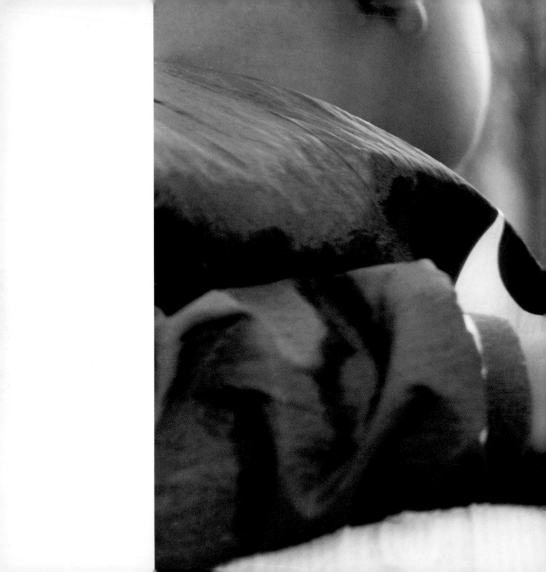

Without a family,
man, alone in the world,
trembles with the cold.

[ANDRE MAUROIS]

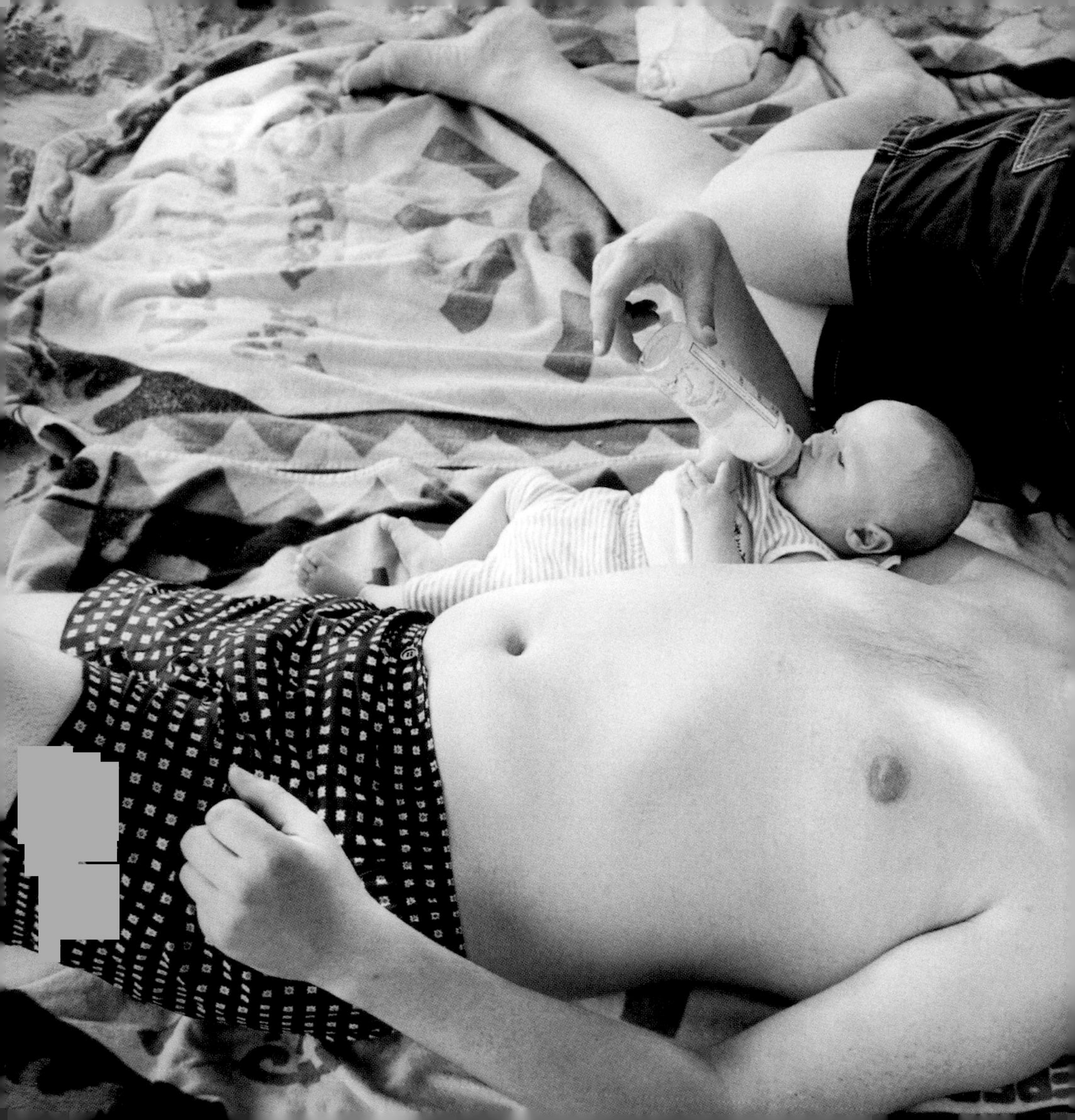

Hold tenderly that which you cherish.

[BOB ALBERTI]

Love is but the discovery
of ourselves in others, and the
delight in the recognition.

[ALEXANDER SMITH]

Seek the wisdom of the ages,

but look at the world through the eyes of a child.

[RON WILD]

The family is one of
nature's **masterpieces**.

[GEORGE SANTAYANA]

Don't walk in front of me,

I may not follow.

Don't walk behind me,

I may not lead.

Just walk beside me
and be my friend.

[ALBERT CAMUS]

Front cover image and pages 4–5
© Shannon Eckstein, Canada
Rubbing noses in Vancouver, Canada – new father Davy finds the perfect way to bond with his baby daughter, Ciara, only nine days old.

Page 2
© Louise Gubb, South Africa
The simple love of a family bonds a father and son beside the Fiherenana River in Madagascar. The Malagasy people come to this area to mine for sapphires.

Page 6
© Pepe Franco, USA
Father-to-be Angel can't help laughing as he tells a joke to his unborn baby. This image of Angel and his partner, Isabel, was captured during a family party in Aguilas, Spain.

Page 8
© Slim Labidi, France
One-month-old Malik is the centre of attention for his loving parents, Cecile and Hafid, photographed at their home in Villeurbaine, France.

Page 9
© Jim Witmer, USA
A photographer father takes a self-portrait with his one-year-old son, Adam, at home in Troy, Ohio, USA.

Pages 10–11
© Henry Hill, USA
Eight-day-old Cyrus is content and secure as he lies sleepily on his father Joe. The young baby had only just left hospital and this image was taken on his first day at home in Colorado Springs, Colorado, USA

Page 13
© Victor Englebert, USA
In the Amazon rainforest of Brazil, a Yanomami Indian relaxes in a hammock made of bark strips and plays with his young grandson.

Page 14
© Madan Mahatta, India
While his parents visit a camel fair in the desert of Rajasthan, India, a young child enjoys the tender love and care of his grandfather.

Page 15
© Jane Wyles, New Zealand
Laughter is infectious for father and son, Drew and James, as they share an affectionate hug in Christchurch, New Zealand.

Pages 16–17
© Kris Allan, UK
Father and son at the Goldstone soccer ground in Hove, England.

Page 19
© John McNamara, USA
The Special Olympics in Union City, California – father Daryl gives his son, JR, a hug full of love and pride after the young competitor finishes his event.

Page 20
© Toshihiro Ogasawara, Japan
Bathtime becomes playtime for Atsuki and his young sons, Yuya, aged one, and Kazuki, three, at the family home in Hyogo, Japan.

Page 21
© Stacey P Morgan, USA
Bathtime story in Chester Springs, Pennsylvania, USA. Five-year-old Devin listens intently to his grandfather reading.

Pages 22–23
© Jeremy Rall, USA
A father lifts up his young son to give him a better view of a street festival in Santa Monica, California, USA.

Pages 24–25
© Maňo Štrauch, Slovak Republic
Outside a Franciscan church in the Slovak Republic, a homeless couple steal a kiss. They are hoping for charitable gifts from the departing congregation. Their three-month-old son, Ivanko, born in an underground cave on the outskirts of the city, yawns as he waits.

Pages 26–27
© Lorenz Kienzle, Germany
A family lies in relaxed contentment on the shore of the River Elbe in Germany.

Pages 28–29
© Martin Rosenthal, Argentina
A father and his children in Juanchaco, Colombia.

Page 30
© Robert Billington, Australia
At the end of the Shark Island swimming race in Sydney, Australia, a one-legged competitor emerges from the surf. His young son hurries over with his artificial limb. This teamwork means his father can run to the finishing line.

Page 31
© Luca Trovato, USA
The Gobi Desert, Mongolia – stranded with all their belongings, a nomadic family are relaxed as they await help.

Page 32

© Marc Rochette, Canada

A look of love and encouragement from father to daughter. Six-year-old Erica's soccer team from Bramalea, Canada, may not win very often, but her father is always on hand to support her efforts in the game.

Pages 34–35

© Dave Marcheterre, Canada

Cheek to cheek – father and daughter hold each other close on a chilly morning in Gaspésie, Quebec, Canada.

Page 36

© Michael Decher, Germany

"Klara and me" – this self-portrait captures a father's face full of tenderness and love as he holds his one-week-old daughter.

Page 37 and back cover image

© Tong Wang, China

A father holds his sleeping child as he cycles through Zhengzhou, China.

Page 38

© Gordon Trice, USA

Father Heath holds his eight-month-old daughter, Bethany. This family portrait was photographed in Abilene, Texas, USA.

Page 39

© Sándor Horváth, Romania

The long road – an elderly man sees that his young relative comes to no harm as they make their way towards a small town in Transylvania, Romania.

Page 40

© Ray Peek, Australia

"Big" Morrie Dingle, a grazier in South Queensland, Australia, and his two grandsons take a break from the saddle to enjoy some food.

Pages 42–43

© Marcy Appelbaum, USA

In Jacksonville, Florida, USA, two-year-old Rachel is curious to see if her belly button matches her father's.

Pages 44–45

© David Williams, UK

Face to face – in Newcastle, England, godfather David meets his one-month-old godson, Samuel, for the first time.

Page 47

© Rajib De, India

Three-year-old Tito follows in the footsteps of an 82-year-old professor on an afternoon stroll through Calcutta, India.

Pages 48–49

© Peter Thomann, Germany

When two-year-old Julian visits his grandparents' house in Emmendingen, Germany, he is fascinated by the smoke from grandfather Ernst's cigar.

Pages 50–51

© Guus Rijven, The Netherlands

Overcoming the generation gap in Brummen, the Netherlands. Eighty-one years separate a grandfather from his only grandchild, but that's no barrier to play. Two-year-old Jarón chooses the game.

Page 52

© Lambro (Tsiliyiannis), South Africa

Two-year-old Robert greets his 85-year-old grandfather, Christy, in Cape Town, South Africa.

Page 53

© Mark Engledow, USA

The photographer's daughter – six-year-old Kitty – stretches on tip-toe to give her grandfather, Bert, a kiss in Bloomington, Indiana, USA.

Pages 54–55

© Stephen Hathaway, UK

Charles and his grandson Richard are deep in conversation as they sit in Soho Square, London, England.

Pages 56–57

© Edmond Terakopian, UK

British Royal Air Force sergeant John has just returned from the Gulf War to his wife, Sharon, and their two-year-old son, Phillip. Their reunion was captured during a press conference in Stanmore, Middlesex, England.

Pages 58–59

© Heather Pillar, Taiwan

Rob Schwartz with his father, Morrie. Mitch Albom, a writer and former student of Morrie, noticed Morrie on a television show and renewed contact with his old professor. The outcome was Albom's moving bestseller *Tuesdays with Morrie*, based on time spent with Morrie on the last 14 Tuesdays of his life.

Page 60-61

© Andrei Jewell, New Zealand

Norbu and his young granddaughter make the most of the warm sunshine in Zanskar in the Indian Himalayas.

Inspired by the 1950s landmark photographic exhibition, *"The Family of Man,"* M.I.L.K. began as an epic global search to develop a collection of extraordinary and geographically diverse images portraying humanity's Moments of Intimacy, Laughter and Kinship (M.I.L.K.). This search took the form of a photographic competition — probably the biggest, and almost certainly the most ambitious of its kind ever to be conducted. With a world-record prize pool, and renowned Magnum photographer Elliott Erwitt as Chief Judge, the M.I.L.K. competition attracted 17,000 photographers from 164 countries. Three hundred winning images were chosen from the over 40,000 photographs submitted to form the basis of the M.I.L.K. Collection.

The winning photographs were first published as three books titled *Family*, *Friendship* and *Love* in early 2001, and are now featured in a range of products worldwide, in eight languages in more than 20 countries. The M.I.L.K. Collection also forms the basis of an international travelling exhibition.

The M.I.L.K. Collection portrays unforgettable images of human life, from its first fragile moments to its last. They tell us that the rich bond that exists between families and friends is universal. Representing many diverse cultures, the compelling and powerful photographs convey feelings experienced by people around the globe. Transcending borders, the M.I.L.K. imagery reaches across continents to celebrate and reveal the heart of humanity.

www.milkphotos.com

First published in Australia in 2003 by Hodder Headline Australia Pty Limited [a member of the Hodder Headline Group], Level 22, 201 Kent Street, Sydney NSW 2000.

First published in New Zealand in 2003 by Hodder Moa Beckett Publishers [a member of the Hodder Headline Group], 4 Whetu Place, Mairangi Bay, Auckland, New Zealand.

Designed by Kylie Nicholls. Printed by Midas Printing Limited, Hong Kong. Back cover quotation by Frederick Buechner.

ISBN 0733617077

MOMENTS INTIMACY LAUGHTER KINSHIP